... 70 Wonderful ...
Word Family Poems

Compiled by Jennifer Wilen and Beth Handa

S C H O L A S T I C
PROFESSIONALBOOKS

NEW YORK • TORONTO • LONDON • AUCKLAND • SYDNEY
MEXICO CITY • NEW DELHI • HONG KONG • BUENOS AIRES

Acknowledgements

"Crunch and Lick" by Dorothy Aldis. From *Is Anybody Hungry?*
by Dorothy Aldis. Copyright 1964 by Dorothy Aldis. Used by permission
of G.P. Putnam's Sons, an imprint of Penguin Putnam Books
for Young Readers, a division of Penguin Putnam Inc.

"Freckles" by Aileen Fisher. From *In One Door and Out the Other*
copyright 1969 by Aileen Fisher.
Reprinted by permission of Marian Reiner for the author.

"Rainy Day" by William Wise, copyright 1971 by William Wise.

"Rice Pudding" by A. A. Milne. From *When We Were Very Young*
by A. A. Milne. Copyright 1924 by E.P. Dutton, renewed 1952 by A. A. Milne.
Used by permission of Dutton Children's Books, an imprint of Penguin Putnam
Books for Young Readers, a division of Penguin Putnam Inc.

"Run A Little" by James Reeves.
From *Read Aloud Poems for the Very Young,* copyright 1952 by James Reeves.

"An Exciting Trip" by Frances Gorman Risser, "Little Squirrel" by Ethel Hopper,
"Grandpa's Clock" by Alice Green, and "Tiny Seeds" by Vera L. Stafford were previously
published in *Poetry Place Anthology,* Scholastic Professional Books, copyright 1983.

Every attempt has been made to secure permissions from the holders of these
copyrights. Any omissions will be corrected in further printings of this book.

■ ■ ■

Cover and interior design by Josué Castilleja
Interior illustration by Maxie Chambliss

ISBN 0-439-20107-1

Printed in the U.S.A.

Contents

Introduction

What do *cat*, *hat*, *sat*, and *bat* have in common? They all belong to the same family—word family, that is. Word families, also known as phonograms, can offer you an efficient way to boost the skills of your early readers.

The beauty of word families lies in the fact that nearly 500 primary-grade words can be derived from a very small set of word families (approximately 36). Another value of word families is that they are reliable and generalizable—most are pronounced and spelled the same in every word in which they appear. Knowing these word families will allow you to get the most out of your phonics instruction. Teaching your students how to recognize these word families will improve their decoding and spelling skills.

Word families have been used in spelling instruction because word patterns are the most effective vehicle for teaching spelling. Word families have also been used to provide a boost to early reading instruction. Many children enter first grade with a fair grasp of consonants and the sounds they represent. By learning a word family such as *-at*, they can generate a number of primary-level words such as *bat*, *cat*, *fat*, *hat*, *mat*, *pat*, *rat*, and *sat*. Students can then use these words in early independent writing. And, children will encounter these words again and again while reading many primary-level stories.

Teaching children that words contain recognizable chunks—and teaching them to search for these word parts or patterns—is an important step in developing reading fluency. As children encounter more and more multisyllabic words, they gain an understanding that words may contain recognizable parts (word families, suffixes, prefixes, smaller words, and so on). This insight is critical for decoding the words quickly and efficiently.

The delightful poems in *70 Wonderful Word Family Poems* make word study playful and engaging. They will enhance your students' understanding of how words work, build reading fluency, and improve their overall literacy skills. Besides…they're a lot of fun!

Enjoy!

Wiley Blevins
Ed.M. Harvard University

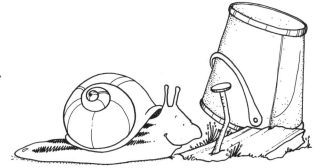

4

Using This Book

The following lesson plan is an easy, systematic way of presenting each poem and using it as a springboard into teaching phonics. You can use this method with individual children, small groups, or the whole class. Also, you can do the lesson in one sitting, or break up the steps so that the poem lasts all week long.

1. Write the poem on chart paper or enlarge it for the entire class to read at once (charts can be laminated for reuse). Poems can also be made into a transparency and shown on an overhead projector.

2. Explain to children that you are going to read a poem that has many words with a certain ending sound, and that they all belong to a group called a *word family*. Point out a word in the poem that has the target word family and underline it.

3. Read the poem aloud for children to enjoy and have children identify the "word family" words. Highlight or underline them in a bold color.

4. Enjoy the poem again, trying some variations:

- Copy the Word Family Treasure Chest on page 80 for each child and have them write each word family word they hear on a line.
- List each word family word on chart paper as you go.
- Have boys and girls alternate reading lines.
- Have a child come up and conduct the class reading the poem.
- Add movement and/or hand motions when reading the poem.
- Cover several words in the poem before the class reads it. Have children supply the words as they read the poem.
- Ask children to listen closely and identify all the word family words (they might raise their hand or clap when they hear one, or you might choose a volunteer to point to the word on the page).
- Write each of the words from the word family on an unlined index card. Use a different color for the rhyme than the rest of the word. Read each word on the cards with the children. Distribute the cards to children and have them hold up their card as their word is read.

5. Last, give each child a copy of the poem to read on their own, color, and enjoy! Invite them to highlight or underline each word family word. They might keep all of their poems in a "Word Family" folder.

70 WONDERFUL WORD FAMILY POEMS Scholastic Professional Books

You might also try the following activities as children become more and more familiar with the poem:

- Brainstorm a list of other words in the word family, modeling how to make words by matching the initial sound with the ending (for instance, -ail: *bail, daily, fail, hail*).

- Give children a mixed-up version of the weekly poem! Children rearrange and then glue the poem in the correct sequence to a blank piece of paper.

- Use the list of word family words as a weekly spelling test.

- Have children fill in cloze sentences with words from the word family.

- Have children illustrate the poem.

- Have partners create crossword puzzles using word family words for each other to solve.

- Make (or have children make) word search puzzles using word family words.

- Invite children to listen to recorded poems at the listening center.

- Write original poems collaboratively using word family words.

- Play "Sounds Like." ("I'm thinking of a word that sounds like *sail* but begins like the word *pudding*.")

- Challenge children to alphabetize the word family words.

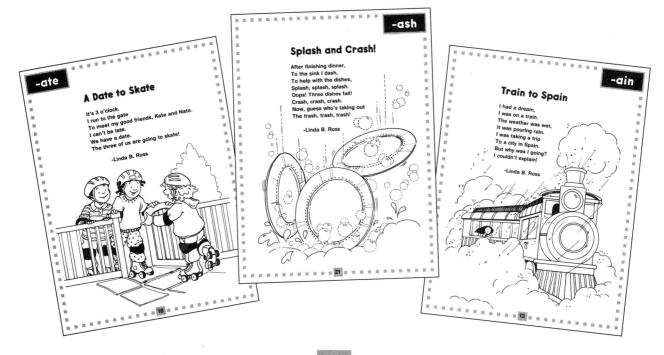

The Most Commonly Found Word Families

-at	-ake	-ash	-an	-ay	-est	-ight	-ick	-in	-ore	-op	-uck
bat	bake	bash	ban	bay	best	fight	kick	bin	bore	bop	buck
cat	cake	cash	can	day	jest	knight	lick	fin	core	cop	duck
fat	fake	dash	Dan	gay	lest	light	Nick	kin	fore	hop	luck
gnat	Jake	gash	fan	hay	nest	might	pick	pin	gore	mop	muck
hat	lake	hash	man	jay	pest	night	quick	tin	more	pop	puck
mat	make	lash	pan	lay	rest	right	Rick	win	pore	sop	suck
pat	quake	mash	ran	may	test	sight	sick	chin	sore	top	tuck
rat	rake	rash	tan	nay	vest	tight	tick	grin	tore	chop	Chuck
sat	sake	sash	van	pay	west	blight	wick	shin	wore	crop	cluck
vat	take	brash	bran	ray	zest	bright	brick	skin	chore	drop	pluck
brat	wake	clash	clan	say	chest	flight	chick	spin	score	flop	stuck
chat	brake	flash	plan	way	crest	fright	click	thin	shore	plop	struck
flat	drake	slash	scan	clay	quest	plight	flick	twin	snore	prop	truck
scat	flake	smash	span	fray	wrest	slight	slick		spore	shop	
slat	shake	stash	than	gray			stick	**-ip**	store	slop	**-ump**
spat	snake	thrash		play			thick	dip	swore	stop	bump
that	stake	trash		spray	**-ink**	**-ine**	trick	hip			dump
			-ack	stay	kink	dine		lip			hump
			back	stray	link	fine	**-ill**	nip	**-oke**	**-ot**	jump
-ail	**-ame**	**-aw**	hack	sway	mink	line	ill	quip	coke	cot	lump
bail	came	caw	Jack	tray	rink	mine	bill	rip	joke	dot	pump
fail	dame	draw	lack		sink	nine	dill	sip	poke	got	rump
Gail	fame	flaw	pack		wink	pine	fill	tip	woke	hot	chump
hail	game	gnaw	quack	**-ell**	blink	vine	gill	zip	yoke	jot	clump
jail	lame	jaw	rack	bell	brink	shine	hill	blip	broke	knot	frump
mail	name	law	sack	cell	clink	shrine	Jill	chip	choke	lot	grump
nail	same	paw	tack	dell	drink	spine	kill	clip	smoke	not	plump
pail	tame	raw	black	fell	shrink	swine	mill	drip	spoke	pot	slump
quail	blame	saw	clack	jell	slink	whine	pill	flip	stoke	rot	stump
rail	flame	straw	crack	Nell	stink		quill	grip	stroke	tot	thump
sail	frame	thaw	knack	sell	think	**-ing**	sill	ship		blot	trump
tail	shame		shack	tell		bing	till	skip		clot	
wail			slack	well	**-ice**	ding	will	slip	**-ock**	plot	
flail		**-ap**	smack	yell	dice	king	chill	snip	dock	shot	**-ug**
frail	**-ate**	cap	snack	dwell	lice	ping	drill	strip	hock	slot	bug
snail	date	gap	stack	shell	nice	ring	frill	trip	knock	spot	dug
trail	fate	map	track	smell	mice	sing	grill	whip	lock	trot	hug
	gate	lap	whack	spell	rice	wing	skill		mock		jug
	hate	nap		swell	vice	zing	spill	**-it**	rock		lug
-ain	Kate	rap			price	bring	still	bit	sock	**-ow**	mug
main	late	sap	**-ank**	**-eat**	slice	cling	thrill	fit	tock	bow	pug
pain	mate	tap	bank	beat	splice	fling	trill	hit	block	cow	rug
rain	rate	yap	Hank	feat	thrice	spring	twill	kit	crock	how	tug
vain	crate	chap	lank	heat	twice	sting		knit	clock	now	chug
brain	grate	clap	rank	meat		string		lit	flock	sow	drug
chain	plate	flap	sank	neat	**-ide**	swing		pit	frock	vow	plug
drain	skate	scrap	tank	peat	hide	thing		quit	shock	brow	shrug
grain	state	slap	yank	seat	ride	wring		sit	smock	chow	slug
plain		snap	blank	bleat	side			wit	stock	plow	smug
slain		strap	clank	cheat	tide			flit			snug
Spain		trap	crank	cleat	wide			grit			thug
sprain		wrap	drank	pleat	bride			skit			
stain			flank	treat	glide			slit			
strain			Frank	wheat	pride			spit			
train			plank		slide			split			
			prank		snide						
			spank		stride						
			thank								

70 WONDERFUL WORD FAMILY POEMS Scholastic Professional Books

Run a Little

Run a little this way,
Run a little that!
Fine new feathers
For a fine new hat.
A fine new hat
For a lady fair—
Run round and turn about
And jump in the air.

Run a little this way,
Run a little that!
White silk ribbon
For a black silk cat.
A black silk cat
For the Lord mayor's wife
Run around and turn about
And fly for your life!

-James Reeves

Mistress Pratt

Mistress Pratt
Round and fat,
By accident sat
Upon her hat.
She squashed it flat
And that was that!

70 WONDERFUL WORD FAMILY POEMS Scholastic Professional Books

Holding Hands

Elephants walking
Along the trails
Are holding hands
By holding tails

Trunks and tails
Are handy things

When elephants walk
On circus rings.

Elephants work
And elephants play

And elephants walk
And feel so gay.

And when they walk—
It never fails

They're holding hands
By holding tails.

-Lenore M. Link

70 WONDERFUL WORD FAMILY POEMS Scholastic Professional Books

Snail Wail

Creeping along the forest trail,
Slowly, slowly crawls a snail.

She has a hard shell and a squishy tail
As she creeps along—her name is Gail.

Exploring the forest, she found an old nail,
And she crawled underneath a rusty pail.

But she couldn't get out and started to wail,
And her mother came and got her on the forest trail.

-Helen O'Reilly

Rice Pudding

What is the matter with Mary Jane?
She is crying with all her might and main,
And she won't eat her dinner—rice pudding again—
What is the matter with Mary Jane?

What is the matter with Mary Jane?
I've promised her dolls and a daisy-chain,
And a book about animals—all in vain—
What is the matter with Mary Jane?

What is the matter with Mary Jane?
She's perfectly well, and she hasn't a pain;
What is the matter with Mary Jane?

What is the matter with Mary Jane?
I've promised her sweets and a ride in the train,
And I have begged her to stop for a bit and explain—
What is the matter with Mary Jane?

What is the matter with Mary Jane?
She's perfectly well and she hasn't a pain,
And it's lovely rice pudding for dinner again
What is the matter with Mary Jane?

-A. A. Milne

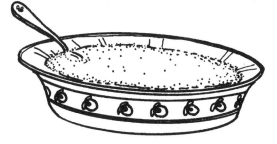

Train to Spain

I had a dream,
I was on a train.
The weather was wet,
It was pouring rain.
I was taking a trip
To a city in Spain.
But why was I going?
I couldn't explain!

-Linda B. Ross

13

Ducks and Drakes

A duck and a drake,
And a halfpenny cake,
With a penny to pay the old baker.

A hop and a scotch
Is another notch,
Slitherum, slatherum, take her.

14

Cinderella

Cinderella, dressed in yella,
Went upstairs to kiss a fella.
Made a mistake and kissed a snake.
How many doctors did it take?

70 WONDERFUL WORD FAMILY POEMS Scholastic Professional Books

-ame

What's Your Name?

What's your name?
Puddin Tame.
Ask me again
And I'll tell you the same.
Where do you live?
In a sieve.
What's your number?
Cucumber!

Oh, What a Shame!

I got sick,
Oh, what a shame.
Now I can't play
In the soccer game.
There's nothing to do.
There's no one to blame.
But all the same,
Oh, what a shame!

-Linda B. Ross

70 WONDERFUL WORD FAMILY POEMS   Scholastic Professional Books

A Date to Skate

It's 3 o'clock.
I run to the gate
To meet my good friends, Kate and Nate.
I can't be late.
We have a date.
The three of us are going to skate!

-Linda B. Ross

Kate the Super-Skate

I have a little sister
My sister's name is Kate.
My speedy little sister
loves to skate, skate, skate.
There's no one who is faster
She really is first-rate,
She's always first to get to school,
She's never, ever late!
My speedy little sister known
as Kate the Super-Skate!

-Helen O'Reilly

19

Dash the Dolphin

There is a dolphin in the sea,
The dolphin's name is Dash.
If you like dolphins (just like me)
You'd love to see him splash.

He splashes when the sea is calm
Or when the waves go crash!
He splishes and he splashes
And he's faster than a flash!

He splashes when the waves go crash.
He splashes when the waves go bash.
He splashes when the waves go smash!
That dolphin they call Dash!

-Helen O'Reilly

70 WONDERFUL WORD FAMILY POEMS Scholastic Professional Books

Splash and Crash!

After finishing dinner,
To the sink I dash,
To help with the dishes,
Splash, splash, splash.
Oops! Three dishes fall!
Crash, crash, crash.
Now, guess who's taking out
The trash, trash, trash!

-Linda B. Ross

21

Dragon Fun

The funniest thing I ever saw
Was a dragon who wore
A ring on his claw.
He lived in a cave
With his Maw and Paw,
Who had a beard on his dragon jaw!
Their dragon beds were made of straw,
And they played all day
On their dragon see-saw!

-Helen O'Reilly

I Saw a Crow

One morning I saw
A crow in a tree
Build a nest out of straw,
And then call out to me.
He called loudly, "Caw, caw!"
So I took out my pad,
And then started to draw,
And the crow seemed quite glad!

-Linda B. Ross

23

Spring Zing

Rustling
rippling
flutter,
flap:
bubbling
billowing
crackle,
crack:
stirring
whirring
slither,
snap:
blowing
flowing
tinkle,
tap:
rolling
tolling
rip,
rap;
singing
ringing
zip,
zap.

-Mimmie Mondschein

70 WONDERFUL WORD FAMILY POEMS Scholastic Professional Books

My Magic Cap

When I get into bed at night
I have a magic cap.
I put it on (but not too tight)
It stays on with a strap.
My dreaming cap
Is blue and white
And when it's on my head,
I snap my fingers
With a snap
And clap my hands
With a slap and a clap
And tap my toes
With a tap, tap, tap.
And dream all through the night.

-Helen O'Reilly

25

A Happy Clan

One day Mom said,
"I have a plan.
Let's take a trip
To see Grandma Jan."
So we got into our yellow van,
And that is how our trip began.

When we arrived,
Gran saw our van.
She smiled and waved
And toward us ran.
Now we are one big, happy clan,
Mom, Dad, and me and Grandma Jan!

-Linda B. Ross

Caveman Dan

Dan, Dan, the clean caveman
Cleans his cave the best he can.
He uses a broom and a rock dust pan,
Dan, Dan, the clean caveman.

Dan has a wife and her name is Nan.
She drives a big rock-moving van,
She cools herself with a paper fan,
Nan, Nan with her moving van.

Dan and Nan have a son named Stan,
He cooks their breakfast in a rock frying pan,
If he can't cook it, nobody can,
Stan, Stan, with his frying pan.

-Helen O'Reilly

27

Mary Mack

Mary Mack
all dressed in black,
with a big, red bow
in the middle of the back.
She carried her lunch
in a purple pack,
and her high-heeled shoes
went clickety clack.

28

Mack the Lumberjack

Mack, Mack, the lumberjack
chops wood all day,
he's got the knack
for piling wood
in the neatest stack

Mack, Mack, the lumberjack
always packs his favorite snack—
fluffy flapjacks in a stack
piled high in his big backpack

HACK, CRACK, WHACK!
he works so hard
he never slacks
till he goes home—
and hits the sack!

-Kama Einhorn

Hank and Frank

Hank and Frank have a wind-up toy store
But at night it becomes a whole lot more!
All the toys, high up on the shelves
Wind up and move all by themselves!
With a crank, crank, crank, and a crank, crank, crank
The fish blows bubbles inside her tank!
The horse gives his hay a yank
The tap dancers tap with a clickety clank!
The boy puts a coin in his piggy bank
The next morning it's so quiet in the store
You'd never know what happened the night before!

-Samantha Berger

30

Hokey Pokey

Hokey Pokey, hanky panky
I'm the king of Rankee-Jankee,
And I'm well, I thank yee.

31

Tiny Seeds

Tiny seeds are everywhere
Out of doors today.
Some have strong though airy wings
To take them far away;
Some in cradles soft and brown
From the trees to Earth drop down,
Seeking for their winter's nap
A soft, dark place to stay.

-Vera L. Stafford

Rainy Day

I do not like a rainy day.
The road is wet, the sky is gray.
They dress me up, from head to toes,
In lots and lots of rubber clothes.
I wish the sun would come and stay.
I do not like a rainy day.

-William Wise

33

Sally at the Seashore

Sally sells seashells by the seashore.
She sells seashells on the seashell shore.
The seashells she sells are seashore shells,
Of that I'm sure.

She sells seashells by the seashore.
She hopes she will sell all her seashells soon.

If neither he sells seashells
Nor she sells seashells,
Who shall sell seashells?
Shall seashells be sold?

34

Where Is Nell?

Where is my kitten, little Nell,
Can you be hiding in the dell?
Please let me know,
I wish you'd tell
Where you are hiding, little Nell.

I think I'll ring the dinner bell,
And put out food for you to smell.
Oh there you are,
No need to yell.
You've come for dinner, little Nell.

-Linda B. Ross

70 WONDERFUL WORD FAMILY POEMS Scholastic Professional Books

Halloween on Silly Street

There is a street in my town
where I went to trick-or-treat.
But instead of candy, I got
Silly things to eat.
One lady gave me lima beans,
One gave me shredded wheat,
One gave me chicken gumbo
and one gave me roasted meat!
I think that was a silly trick,
and not a tasty treat!

-Helen O'Reilly

A Treat to Eat

Mom said, "Get ready for a treat."
It would be something good to eat.
It wasn't cheese or fish or meat.
It wasn't made from flour or wheat.
It was my favorite fruit—how neat!
A bowl of cherries—what a treat!

-Linda B. Ross

37

A Little Guest

Beneath a tree,
As I lay and rest,
A little bird
Fell on my chest.
"Hello!" I said
To my little guest,
And I took him up
To his little nest.

-Linda B. Ross

70 WONDERFUL WORD FAMILY POEMS Scholastic Professional Books

My Brother Is a Sailor

My brother is a sailor
He sails from east to west.
He wears a sailor suit with lots
of medals on his chest.
He's busy on his sailing ship,
He has no time to rest,
He loves to travel on the sea,
But he loves home the best.

-Helen O'Reilly

39

I Think

To fly a shiny rocket ship,
that's what I'd like, I think.
Away from earth I'd slide and slip
Past stars that wink and blink.
(I'd have to bring some food with me
And also juice to drink!)
I'd fly so high into the sky
the earth would seem to shrink!
then
I'd write a book about my trip
with a special pen and ink.

-Helen O'Reilly

40

'Round the Rink

As I skate slowly 'round the rink,
So nervous and scared
I can't even blink,
Two skaters breeze past me,
As quick as a wink.
"I'll skate like that someday.
I'll do it!" I think.

-Linda B. Ross

41

Freckles

Jerry has freckles,
Peppered like spice.

And Jerry has a pony
I rode on twice.

I think freckles
are awfully nice.

-Aileen Fisher

Mice Advice

Let me give you
This advice:
Think twice
When you see mice—
Some people find them scary,
But they're not!
They're really rather nice,
You can feed them bits of rice,
Or some birthday cake—
(A slice, but not a lot!)

-Helen O'Reilly

43

Side By Side

When we're at the park,
There's a lot to decide!
Should we toss a ball?
Should we ride or slide?
Or maybe we should play and hide,
Or swing together side by side.

-Linda B. Ross

I Like to Ride

The playground is the place for my friend and me,
It's full of things to ride.
We can wobble on the see-saw
Or go swooping down the slide,
We can climb the jungle gym all day
Or use the swings to glide,
And talk about it afterwards
As we walk home side by side.

-Helen O'Reilly

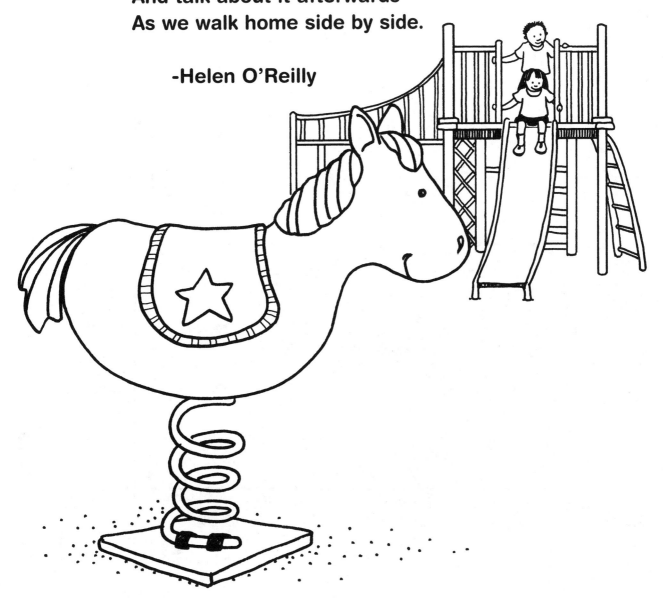

45

Night, Knight

"Night, night,"
said one knight
to the other knight
the other night.
"Night, night, knight."

-Anonymous

Night, Night!

You've no need to light a night-light
On a light night like tonight.
For a night-light's light's a slight light,
And tonight's a night that's light.
When a night's light, like tonight's light,
It is really not quite right.
To light night-lights with their slight lights
On a light night like tonight.

Queen Caroline

Queen, Queen Caroline,
Dipped her hair in turpentine;
Turpentine made it shine,
Queen, Queen Caroline.

70 WONDERFUL WORD FAMILY POEMS Scholastic Professional Books

Engine Engine Number Nine

Engine, engine, number nine,
Gliding down Chicago line;
When she's polished she will shine,
Engine, engine number nine.

Sing for Spring

Sing, bird, sing!
Do you know what your song can bring?
Your music can bring us the season of spring!
With a chirp from your mouth and a flap of your wing
The wintery air will be all full of zing,
Bloom will come to everything,
And I can play all day on my swing.
So sing, bird, sing!

-Kama Einhorn

50

Spring

What do you like about spring?
Can you name more than one thing?
I like the birds by my window that sing.
I like the sweet smells that flowers can bring.
I like to daydream and sit on a swing.
That's what I like about spring!

-Linda B. Ross

Crunch and Lick

Popcorn crunches.
Peanuts do.
The cone part of an ice-cream cone
Is wonderful for crunching too.

Things to lick are candy sticks.
Rainbow-colored popsicles.
Chocolate sauce when it begins
To leak and trickle
Down our chins.

-Dorothy Aldis

A Chick Trick

An egg can be the home
Of a tiny baby chick.
And when it's time to hatch, the chick
Can do a super trick.
Inside the egg the chick begins
To pick, pick, pick.
You can hear him if you listen,
Going
Click, click, click.
And pretty soon, what do you know?
(It happens pretty quick!)
The chick that was inside the egg
is outside—what a trick!

-Helen O'Reilly

70 WONDERFUL WORD FAMILY POEMS Scholastic Professional Books

Bugs at Home

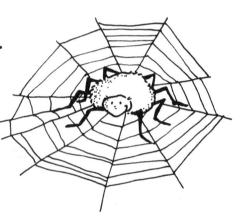

There once was a tick
Whose name was Tock,
He made his home
Beneath a rock.

There once was a bee
Whose name was Clive,
He made his home
Inside a hive.

There once was a spider
Whose name was Jeb,
He made his home
Out of a web.

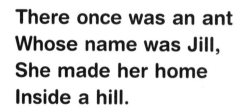

There once was an ant
Whose name was Jill,
She made her home
Inside a hill.

Rock, hive, web, hill,
You can believe me or not as you will.
If they're not gone, they're living there still,
Tock, Clive, Jeb and Jill!

-Helen H. Moore

54

At My Windowsill

Early in the morning,
When all is still,
I sit and wait
At my windowsill,
And watch the sun
Come over the hill,
To paint the sky
With beauty and skill.

-Linda B. Ross

55

Rin Tin Tin

**Rin Tin Tin
Swallowed a pin.
Went to the doctor,
The doctor wasn't in.
He opened the door
And fell on the floor
And that was the end
Of Rin Tin Tin.**

My Twinny Twin

I can point
To my chinny, chin, chin.
I can touch my finger
To my shinny, shin, shin.
I can count the freckles
On my skinny, skin, skin
And I can twirl around with
A spinny, spin, spin.
I can fix a button
With a pinny, pin, pin
And I can do it all
With my twinny, twin, twin.

-Helen O'Reilly

An Exciting Trip

I ride the elevator up
  In our apartment house
And no one knows I'm playing
  For I'm a quiet mouse.

But I pretend I'm piloting
  A rocket, swift as light,
That's full of passengers I'll land
  Upon the Moon tonight.

When we ride down, my rocket ship
  Falls like a shooting star,
And lands upon the earth again
  Without the slightest jar.

The other people never know,
  As up and down we flip,
That I am taking them upon
  A wild, exciting trip!

-Frances Gorman Risser

70 WONDERFUL WORD FAMILY POEMS Scholastic Professional Books

A Dip in the Ocean

I dreamed I owned
A grand old ship,
And with my crew,
I took a trip.
Along came a storm
To tip our ship,
And into the ocean,
We took a dip!

-Linda B. Ross

70 WONDERFUL WORD FAMILY POEMS Scholastic Professional Books

My Dog Kit

I have a dog.
Her name is Kit.
She goes where I go.
She sits where I sit.
My Aunt Sarah,
Who likes to knit,
Made matching sweaters
For me and Kit.
We wear our sweaters,
Oh, what a good fit!
Now when we go walking,
We make quite a hit!

-Linda B. Ross

70 WONDERFUL WORD FAMILY POEMS   Scholastic Professional Books

The Joke You Just Told

The joke you just told isn't funny one bit.
It's pointless and dull, wholly lacking in wit.
It's so old and stale, it's beginning to smell!
Besides, it's the one I was going to tell.

-Anonymous

70 WONDERFUL WORD FAMILY POEMS Scholastic Professional Books

At the Shore

There's nothing I like more
Than swimming at the shore,
Till my arms and legs are sore.
There's nothing I like more.

There's nothing I like more
Than the seashore to explore,
With its sand and shells galore.
There's nothing I like more.

-Linda B. Ross

70 WONDERFUL WORD FAMILY POEMS Scholastic Professional Books

How Barney Lost His Snore

Bears hibernate in wintertime
(you may have heard before).

There was a bear named Barney,
and he could really snore!

It bothered all his neighbors,
so they went to the store,

And chipped in for a bottle of
some stuff called Snore-No-More!

They said, "We love you Barney, but
It's really quite a bore.
To listen to you every year—
our ears are getting sore!"

"I didn't mean it," Barney said,
"It must have been a chore!
But now that you've all helped me out,
I won't snore anymore!"

-Helen O'Reilly

-oke

Speak to Me

Speak to me, darlin',
  Oh, speaky, spikey, spokey
Why are those tears
  On my cheeky, chikey, chokey?
Give me the answer
  I seeky, sikey, sokey!
Or else I'll go jump
  In the creeky, crikey, crokey.

64

The Quietest Boy

A boy was so quiet
That when he spoke,
He made no more noise
Than a puff of smoke.
But then one day
I told him a joke
And he laughed so loud
I thought he might choke!
And after that,
Whenever he spoke,
He always told
That funny old joke.

-Helen O'Reilly

65

Grandpa's Clock

"Now, go to bed,"
Says Grandpa's clock
"Tick-tock, tick-tock,
Tick-tock, tick-tock!"
So I put down my big red block,
And then pull off each wrinkled sock.

-Alice F. Green

What Do You Need?

To build a house
You need a block
To tell the time
You need a clock
To open the door
You need to knock,
To sail a ship
You need a dock.
And to cover your foot,
You need a sock.
Block, clock,
Tick tock,
Knock, dock
Sock!

-Helen O'Reilly

Popcorn

Pop, pop, popcorn,
popping in the pot!
Pop, pop, popcorn,
eat it while it's hot!

Pop, pop, popcorn,
butter on the top!
When I eat popcorn,
I can't stop!

-Helen H. Moore

68

My Shop

I like to pretend
I own a shop
That's filled with food
From bottom to top,
Where all the people like to stop
To buy fruit or bread or soda pop.

At the end of the day,
I clean my shop
From top to bottom
And bottom to top.
I hop around with a giant mop,
And when I'm finished, down I flop!

-Linda B. Ross

69

One Cool Tot

One sunny, sunny summer day
When I was just a tot,
The weather was so warm that I got
Very, very, very hot.
I felt hot in my bathtub,
I felt hot in my cot.
Do you think I was happy?
I can tell you,
I was not!
I wished I had some ice cream
I wished for it a lot,
So I could eat it up and be
A real, cool tot.

-Helen O'Reilly

70

Tea Party

One night while I was lying down
Lying in my cot
My dolls thought I was sleeping
But really I was not.

They thought they'd have a party
They used my best teapot
They made themselves some sandwiches
With jelly, apricot.

They smiled at each other
Said "please" and "thanks a lot"
And "would you please pass another spot
Of tea from that teapot?"

-Helen O'Reilly

70 WONDERFUL WORD FAMILY POEMS Scholastic Professional Books

Little Squirrel

A little squirrel runs up and down
   In our old walnut tree.
All day he carries nuts away,
   As busy as can be.
Mother says he stores them safe
   For food when north winds blow;
I wonder how the squirrel knows
   That someday there'll be snow.

-Ethel Hopper

70 WONDERFUL WORD FAMILY POEMS Scholastic Professional Books

Winter Show

What do you know!
It's beginning to snow.
You can hear the wind blow.
And the snowdrifts will grow.

What do you know!
The temperature is low.
Big snowballs we'll throw
In this winter white show.

-Linda B. Ross

70 WONDERFUL WORD FAMILY POEMS Scholastic Professional Books

Huckleberry Pie

H, U, uckle
B, U, buckle
H, U, uckle, Y,
H, U, uckle,
B, U, buckle,
HUCKLEBERRY PIE!

Woodchuck Poem

How much wood would a woodchuck chuck
If a woodchuck could chuck wood?
A woodchuck would chuck as much wood
As a woodchuck could chuck
If a woodchuck could chuck wood.

70 WONDERFUL WORD FAMILY POEMS Scholastic Professional Books

Young Roger and Dolly

Young Roger came tapping at
    Dolly's window,
    Thumpaty, thumpaty, thump!

He asked for admittance; she
    Answered him "No!"
    Frumpaty, frumpaty, frump!

"No, no, Roger, no!
    As you came you may go!"
    Stumpaty, stumpaty, stump!

70 WONDERFUL WORD FAMILY POEMS Scholastic Professional Books

Watching Elephants Jump

Look at the elephants,
Large and plump.
I like to watch the elephants jump.
Can you hear them?
Thump, thump, thump!
Elephants jumping over a stump!

-Linda B. Ross

70 WONDERFUL WORD FAMILY POEMS   Scholastic Professional Books

Mr. Ladybug

A ladybug went to work one day,
And said to her husband,
"Now while I'm away,
please take care of the house,
and sweep the floor,
and don't let the baby bugs
fly out the door!"
So he polished, and cleaned, and vacuumed the rug,
he fed all the baby bugs, gave each a hug,
and when he had finished, he said with a shrug,
"It's really hard, being a man ladybug!
Oh, I work, and I work, just as hard as I can,
'Cause it's really hard, being a ladybug man!"

-Helen H. Moore

78

What I Saw

Did you ever see a bug
Drinking coffee from a mug?
Drinking coffee from a mug and going
Glug, glug, glug?
I did!
Did you ever see a bug
Give another bug a hug?
Give another bug a hug and going
Hug, hug, hug?
I did!
Did you ever see a bug
Do a dance upon a rug?
Do a dance upon a rug and going
chug, chug, chug?
I did!

-Helen O'Reilly

79

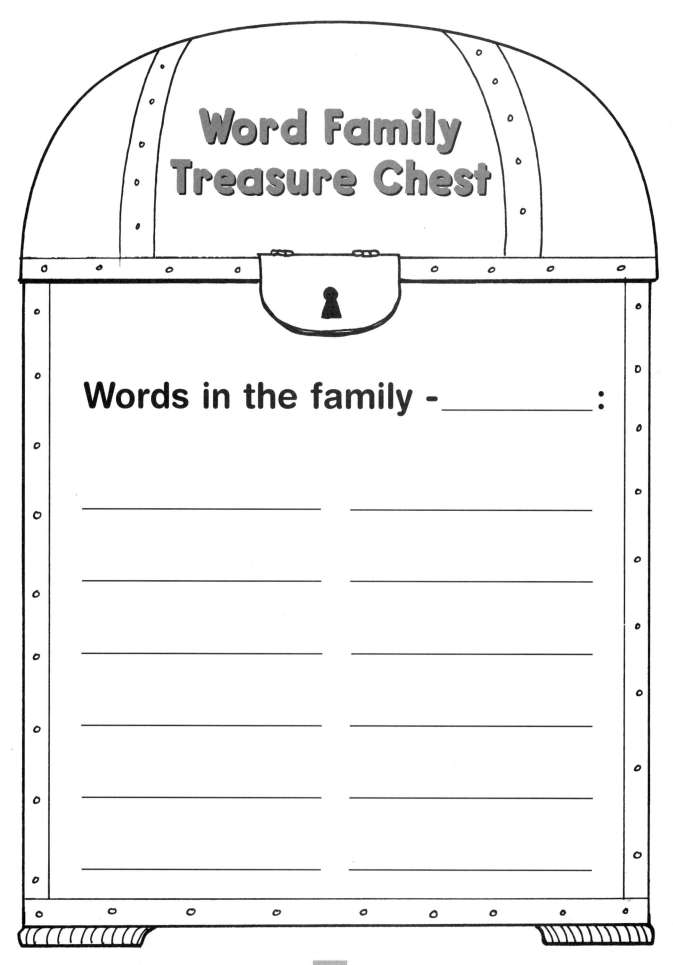

Word Family Treasure Chest

Words in the family - _____ :

_____   _____

_____   _____

_____   _____

_____   _____

_____   _____

70 WONDERFUL WORD FAMILY POEMS Scholastic Professional Books